MASTER HMO'S TODAY,
CHANGE YOUR LIFE
FOREVER

101 Questions and Answers
Relating to HMOs

By CJ Haliburton, the leading writer, trainer and

authority on how to multi-let property

HMO Daddy
14 Walsall Road
Wednesbury
West Midlands
WS10 9JL

Print Edition
ISBN 978-1-326-46938-2
British Library Cataloguing in Publication Data.
A catalogue record for this book is available from the British Library.
Cover design and typesetting by Oxford Literary Consultancy.

CONTENTS

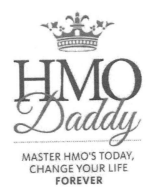

MASTER HMO'S TODAY,
CHANGE YOUR LIFE
FOREVER

WARNING

Jim Haliburton, known as the HMO Daddy, is not a lawyer or financial advisor nor does the following represent legal or financial advice. If legal or financial advice is needed than the reader should seek the appropriate avenues. The following information is given to the best of Jim Halliburton's knowledge as correct, though the reader should make their own enquiries.

INTRODUCTION

Hi, I'm Jim Haliburton, also known as the HMO Daddy as I have acquired over 140 HMOs and 30 single lets. I have more than 900 tenants and am still acquiring property. I don't say this to boast but to show my experience. One of my passions is running training courses teaching people about HMOs, and I have written many leading books and manuals on the subject. I just love sharing my experience.

Welcome to the first edition of 101 Questions and Answers on HMOs. This book has been produced as a result of answering questions asked by those thinking of becoming HMO landlords and landlords both new and advanced.

If there is something you require explaining in more depth, please do not hesitate to contact a member of my team at HMO Daddy and they will be happy to help.

I sincerely hope you find the answers you are looking for in this book and that you gain extra knowledge.

Enjoy

C J Haliburton

November 2015

jim@hmodaddy.com

ACKNOWLEDGEMENT

I would like to thank all the HMO landlords and the people who are thinking about getting into the industry for their questions because this has made this book one of the easiest for me to write. All I had to do was ask my assistant, Rachel Tonks, to pull out all of the questions I have been asked over the years. She categorised them, and when they reached 101 we decided to print them, with a few more that arrived in the meantime. I would like to thank Rachel Tonks for typing up the manuscript. At the rate things are going I will soon be producing another 'More 101 Questions and Answers Relating to HMOs'

I'm just glad that I followed one of the rules that I made early in business and kept a copy of all your letters (now emails) and my replies; this made writing this book very easy.

I have found certain topics keep being repeated for which there is no simple quick answer, so I have recently covered these in my book 'Top Ten Current Issues For HMO Landlords', available from hmodaddy.com.

Can I also thank Piers Benton, Sue Bellamy, Will Donaldson and Jeremy Ngaw for proof reading the original Question and Answer manuscript as well as Claire Williams for her editing and suggestions.

I would like to thank Gary Bees for suggesting the title.

PREFACE

The great difficulty I have found in writing this book is explaining to HMO landlords the enormous variation councils and council officials take on the standards or laws they choose to enforce. Including what is legally required for an HMO, and what the council could do, if you refused, or, worse, whether they would prosecute you if you failed to comply with specific regulations. No landlord seeks confrontation with either the council or tenants. We are in a service industry and looking after the welfare and safety of our tenants is amongst our top priorities. However, on any risk benefit analysis, most of what councils demand serves no benefit to the tenant, is often not wanted, and is sometimes abused. In addition, landlords themselves can often be their own enemy by providing what they think the tenant wants. They often say that they would not provide a house that they themselves would not live in – sorry, but you are not the tenant! I estimate that billions of pounds are wasted every year by councils demanding unnecessary alterations or additions to HMOs and landlords providing what tenants do not expect.

As an HMO landlord, you need to be able to deal with an inconsistent and often illogical approach taken by some councils. I look upon it as a tax for being an HMO landlord: know when to give in and when it is commercially viable to fight. Little of what councils demand can actually be enforced. The vagaries of enforcement often leave me feeling like I am living with an unexploded bomb in my back garden. No landlord should have to put up with such abuse but unfortunately this can be the situation with some councils. Luckily, most councils I deal with are reasonable and are as appalled as I am at how other councils behave.

You will therefore appreciate why I have included a lot of 'may', 'could' and 'possibly' into my answers. If a council was so minded they could, by overzealous enforcement (though they would say they were just enforcing the law), make operating HMOs unviable. Why some councils are so against providing low cost flexible housing is a mystery. Some people just need to have someone to hate, and with all the antidiscrimination legislation, it often seems the only people left to persecute are motorists, dogs, students and landlords. Unfortunately, there is no one out there to protect you. As an HMO landlord, you have to make your own way. I hope my book helps you understand the business better and I wish you every success.

C J HALIBURTON

November 2015

MASTER HMO'S TODAY,
CHANGE YOUR LIFE
FOREVER

I WANT TO HEAR FROM YOU

As a reader of the first edition of 101 Questions and Answers Relating to HMO, you are the most important critic and commentator. I value your opinion and comments. I want to know what else you would like me to include in the book, what you disagree with, and any other words of wisdom you wish me to share.

I would like feedback from you, my readers, both positive and negative. Any improvements I can incorporate to help other landlords through the maze of being an HMO landlord will be gratefully received and I am sure attract the gratitude of landlords I pass them onto.

I welcome your comments and you can email or write to me to let me know what you did or didn't like about my book, as well as what I can do to make it better or what other information or service I could provide.

I also provide training courses on all aspects of the business, which you can find out about on my website hmodaddy.com.

When you write to me, please include your name, email address, home address and phone number. I assure you I will value and review all of your comments.

Jim Haliburton

Email: jim@hmodaddy.com

Website: www.hmodaddy.com

Mail: Jim Haliburton
                14 Walsall Road
                Wednesbury
                WS10 9JL

BASICS

1. Question: What is an HMO?

Answer: An HMO (House in Multiple Occupation, also known as a multi-let or shared house) is one of the many misunderstood aspects of the property business. Many landlords say they operate shared houses or multi-lets and not HMOs, or say that as they haven't fitted locks to doors or adapted the property that it is not an HMO. WRONG: if there are three or more unrelated persons living in the property then it is an HMO. Just because your council takes no notice of small HMOs (and I agree with this), it does not change the wide definition of what an HMO is.

There is also the problem of when a building is an HMO – a house or a flat that has been converted into flats without building control consent, often referred to as 'poorly converted flats', which are classified as HMOs even though there is no sharing. In most areas there are very little extra standards imposed on 'poorly converted' flats.

2. Question: Is an HMO legal?

Answer: Many people think setting up a HMO needs permission and without this it is illegal – WRONG. No permission is needed for a two storey HMO with six (maybe slightly more) tenants. The exception is in areas where Article 4 or where selective or additional licensing applies (see Questions 38, 39 and 44 and you can ask your council or go to their website to see if these apply). However, you must ensure your HMO is safe and complies with the relevant regulations.

3. Question: Is there a limit on how many people I can have in an HMO?

Answer: As long as all the size, legal and safety requirements are met and the house is big enough to accommodate your tenants, then you can have up to six people staying there (maybe slightly more – see my book HMOs and Planning available from hmodaddy.com).

4. Question: How many people are allowed to share a communal bathroom?

Answer: Up to five tenants are allowed to share one communal bathroom. If your council insist you provide more than one bathroom to five tenants you can challenge it – see the answer to Question 51 below.

5. Question: How many people are allowed to share a communal kitchen?

Answer: Five tenants are allowed to share one communal kitchen, although some councils demand more. If they insist you provide more, you can challenge it – see the answer to Question 51 below.

6. Question: Is a communal kitchen compulsory?

Answer: No, each tenant can have their own kitchen, although if there are no shared facilities you may have problems with planners as it may be considered that you have turned the property into flats, which requires planning permission – see my book on HMOs and planning available at hmodaddy.com.

7. Question: If a house has five/six self-contained units, with all unrelated people occupying, is it still an HMO?

Answer: One of the definitions of a HMO is a house or flat which has been converted into separate units, does not have building control approval or comply with building control standards as of 1991, and is not mainly owner-occupied. However, most of the standards that apply to ordinary HMOs do not apply to those units often referred to as 'poorly converted flats'.

8. Question: How do I find a property that I can use as an HMO?

Answer: Once you know what you are looking for, you will be surprised at how often you see properties that are suitable to use as an HMO when you are out and about; driving, commuting or listening to people. I recommend you stick to the area you live in when looking as this makes it easier to manage. If you are looking for a big HMO, often known as a 'mega HMO', then look for spaces above rows of shops, old nursing homes, offices, doctors surgeries, or other redundant commercial buildings. Average HMOs are ideally houses on the end of a row, in a rundown area or industrial estate, and located close to the town centre. Avoid situating an HMO next to other owner-occupied residential properties as this will upset the neighbours. Would you want to live next to an HMO? You may also consider buying a readymade

HMO although they are often expensive and you would normally do far better by making your own.

9. Question: Does an HMO have to include a shared lounge/sitting room or can I rent it out as an additional bedroom?

Answer: You don't need to provide a shared lounge or sitting room, but you do need to think about what your tenants want. It's also important to keep in mind that some councils require larger bedrooms if you don't supply a shared lounge or dining kitchen. With the lower end of the market, lounges can cause problems as tenants occasionally invite people to stay in them, or they use them to store things, or they get together and cause a nuisance.

10. Question: Do you still need a communal kitchen and/or a communal bathroom in a self-contained HMO?

Answer: If you make the rooms self-contained, I would refer to the kitchen area contained within the rooms as 'tea-making facilities' and provide a shared kitchen. This helps prevent issues with planning the self-contained rooms could be classified as flats and they may not meet the necessary standards for flats as, amongst other things, the rooms would not be big enough. Without a shared facility, the planners could demand that you apply for retrospective planning permission. You may also find that each room will attract a separate Council Tax band, i.e. each self-contained room will have to pay Council Tax. (See Question 54)

11. Question: How many communal areas should there be in an HMO?

Answer: An HMO does not have to have any communal areas. Again, this is one of the many misunderstandings about HMOs: see Questions 6, 7, 9 and 10 above.

12. Question: What should a shared kitchen include? For example, should the kitchen include a washing machine, oven, hob, table and chairs or dishwasher?

Answer: The easiest way to deal with this is to go online and see what your council demands but, more importantly, what your tenants want. There are no specific requirements for you to provide a washing machine or dishwasher, and the need for a table and chairs is questionable. By law, an HMO landlord needs to provide a sink, drainer, running hot and cold water, cooker, fridge and storage. On the topic of storage, many councils overlook the need for this, accepting that in a shared house if you leave anything out it can get stolen. On the other hand, some councils are obsessed with storage, drainers and work surface space. The easiest way to make sure you have all the necessary requirements is to go online and see what your council demands. However, more importantly, you should think about what your tenants require.

13. Question: Must the kitchen have a fire extinguisher or fire blanket? Should these be provided anywhere else in the HMO, e.g. hallways?

Answer: It depends on the council. Most demand fire blankets in kitchens. Fire extinguishers are a contentious issue, as some say you need to be trained to use them so they do not require them to be provided; or if you do, you must train your tenants how to use them.

14. Question: Where should the kitchen be located? (In a three storey HMO)

Answer: Again, this is down to the council. Some demand the kitchen to be no more than one floor away, so it should be on the first floor of a three storey building. Most will accept a kitchen anywhere providing there are dining facilities nearby, i.e. somewhere the tenants can sit and eat situated close to the kitchen. If you provide kitchenettes in each room then often little notice is taken of the communal kitchen, providing the kitchenettes are sufficient.

15. Question: Am I allowed to put two people in a double bedroom or am I only allowed one person per room?

Answer: Most councils operate to space standards which say that a room must have 65 sq. ft. (6.5 sq. m) per one person, 100 sq. ft. (10 sq. m) for two people, and so on. Generally having two people in a double bedroom is fine however, you should be careful of couples as they tend to cause problems.

16. Question: Is there a minimum stay period I have to give my tenants who want to rent a room?

Answer: There is no simple answer to this. The same rights of occupation (also known as security of tenure) apply to room lets as apply to houses and flats. Many landlords find this surprising, but it is the law. You can grant a tenancy for any period, but the minimum period a tenant is entitled to stay is six months, though they can leave after the period you grant. For example, you can offer a week–to-week or month-to-month tenancy and the tenant can leave after one week or month. Where it gets difficult is if the tenant does not leave or does not pay. I cover this in my manual 'DIY EVICTION' and 'HMOs and Compensation for Unlawful Eviction'.

You are unable to bring eviction proceedings against a tenant for six months (longer if you granted a longer tenancy) unless they have broken their tenancy agreement.

Once a tenant is in occupation, they can stay indefinitely until you serve on them what is called a Section 21 Notice and make an application to the court to get a possession order. If the tenant still refuses to leave, a court bailiff must do it for you.

17. Question: Do all tenants in the same HMO have to be from the same category e.g. unemployed or working?

Answer: There is no law regarding this. I now try and keep all tenants in each HMO in the same category – professional, working, students and unemployed – and in the same age range, as this reduces disagreements. Without appearing to be stereotypical, each category usually has a completely different way of life, for example; unemployed tenants tend to sleep in and go to bed very late, while professionals will be out working all day and asleep all night. Young tenants tend to socialise more and be noisy.

18. Question: Is there a maximum number of units you can have in one HMO?

Answer: Yes and no. As long as there is enough room and each room complies to size standards (see Question 15) it should not be a problem. However, once you have over six tenants living in an HMO then you may require planning permission. In an Article 4 area (see Question 44), you need planning permission if you have more than two unrelated tenants.

19. Question: Should you have a set of rules for your tenants to follow?

Answer: Yes, it is a legal requirement that you manage your HMO, and part of this, I believe, is ensuring as far as you can that tenants behave well. For my set of rules, see my useful manual 'HMO landlord forms and letters', available from hmodaddy.com.

20. Question: Can I situate a bedroom next to a communal kitchen?

Answer: If in order to exit the bedroom you need to go through the kitchen, this is not a good idea as the kitchen is considered a high fire risk and so the occupant(s) could be trapped in the bedroom in the event of a kitchen fire. It may be allowed depending on the approach of your council. In my area, you can situate a bedroom next to a communal kitchen if they are on the ground floor, though the council may want to see an escape window in the bedroom. It is also allowed on the first floor but my councils always want escape windows in the bedroom. I have never tried to have a kitchen on a second floor so I am not sure what the approach would be, but I think my councils wouldn't allow it.

21. Question: What furniture should I provide in a HMO, if anything?

Answer: Oddly, there is no legal requirement to provide any furniture in a tenant's room. Some HMO landlords who house unemployed tenants don't supply any furniture because local charities will provide it for free to those 'in need'. There is a requirement to provide cooking facilities, see answer to Question 12 above, so while you don't need to provide a bed, you do have to provide cooking facilities. The absurdity of this is that most of my tenants do not cook but they all sleep.

22. Question: Will a property in which a landlord lives with other occupants be classified as an HMO?

Answer: Yes, once you have over two lodgers/tenants. However, most councils do not take any action or interest in such properties.

23. Question: Should the rent include ALL bills? If so, how much will utilities typically cost for a four, five or six bedroom HMO?

Answer: No. The landlord can decide what they would prefer to do, or more importantly what their tenants will accept. By law, the landlord is responsible for the Council

Tax bill if the property is classified as an HMO, but there is nothing to stop the landlord making it a contractual obligation for the tenants to pay. I know a lot of landlords who insist the tenants pay all the bills. I generally pay all the bills in my HMOs, though I am experimenting with different approaches. After an exhaustive analysis of the utility bills for the hundred or so HMOs I have owned over ten years, I can distinguish no difference in cost between a four bed and an eight bed. On average, if you pay all the bills – electric, gas, water and Council Tax – it averages about £3,600 per annum or £300 per calendar month for up to an eight bed HMO. A smaller HMO cots the same to run. Understand this is an average and actual cost can vary. Larger HMOs cost more to operate, but there is little correlation with the number of occupants in an HMO and the cost of the utilities.

24. Question: Do the tenants need to sign individual tenancy agreements/licences or are all to be named on one single agreement?

Answer: It is up to you as the landlord. Apart from students, it is unusual to have all the tenants sign one agreement.

25. Question: How much does it cost to convert a property into an HMO?

Answer: I estimate it costs £6k a room and £12k a studio, with en suite and kitchenette, for a full refurbishment. This usually includes rewiring, re-plumbing and re-plastering. I have however, with a suitable house, converted it into an HMO for a few hundred pounds. A lot is down to what your council demands you do.

HMO – GETTING STARTED

26. Question: I would like a substantial HMO that creates a good income, if that is possible. What type of building should I look for?

Answer: Depending on the rent, it is possible to get exceptional income from an HMO if it is large and purchased at the right price. I look for commercial buildings, flats above a row of shops, a doctor's surgery or rundown pubs. Remember, the more rundown the better: it costs about the same to renovate but more importantly it is usually cheaper to buy. The profit you get depends on the cost of the building: if you borrow the money, it will lower the borrowing costs or, if you have the money, it will give a higher ROI. I look for properties that cost about £10k or less per unit. For example, I look for a building that will give me

of £150k or less. After

near Birmingham, give a

nimum of eight or more

e more units, the more

vn capital do I need to

lio?

y you have the better: you will be able to build your own portfolio faster by buying for cash. If you have only a small amount of money then this can slow you down, as you are usually reliant on remortgaging to get money to buy the next deal. Even the rent-to-rent, lease options, delayed completions and vendor finance options still require some money for the deposit and a first month's rent to the owner plus the cost of turning the property into an HMO. Another option doing a Joint Venture, where an investor provides upfront cash that will cost you either interest or an ongoing share of the profit. You can do a combination of the above to move yourself forward faster, though most investors I have come across tend to use only one strategy.

28. Question: I am struggling to get my first HMO, what am I doing wrong?

Answer: Without speaking to you and knowing more I don't know why. Of all the people new to the industry I have spoken to who experience difficulties in getting going, unless they're in an area of high property prices and comparatively low rents then their problems come down to lack of knowledge, commitment, or the ability to take risks. It's usually the latter issue which prevents most. HMO Daddy offers mentorships that can help you to get you started. We work with you to help you build up your own portfolio. See my website hmodaddy.com for more information.

29. Question: What are the advantages of an HMO over a single let?

Answer: An HMO can be a number of things. In this instance I'm referring to dividing the property up and charging by the room rather than charging for a whole property. The property does not have to be anything special; I have successfully converted two-bedroom-terraced houses into HMOs. You also have the advantage that you can use properties as HMOs which would not let as a house (for example because there is no garden) and these are often cheaper to buy than a house of the same size, for example, an old pub or offices. The rent received by doing this can be as much as five times or more the rent achieved by letting the property as a whole to one tenant. However, there is a lot more regulation on HMOs and usually there is more work involved, though this varies with the type of tenant you house. The unemployed are generally more troublesome but easier to find whereas workers and professionals are straightforward to deal with.

30. Question: What are the disadvantages of an HMO over a single let?

Answer: None, I believe, but I would say that. The general view is that they are much harder to operate, require greater knowledge, and are far more regulated; this is all true, but once you have mastered running an HMO, it is a piece of cake. Manage your properties and do your own maintenance and you have eliminated most of your problems.

31. Question: How do I check if my area is good for HMOs?

Answer: The usual advice is to try a test advertisement and see if it works. However, I am not sure if that is relevant as I find everything lets eventually, usually to the unemployed. I know it appears reckless to say this, but just try it. To minimise risk, try a rent-to-rent with a short break clause rather than buying.

32. Question: How do you go about remortgaging an HMO?

Answer: Same as with a buy to let, except:

(i) You need a buy to let lender who will accept HMOs. A lot do but are restrictive as to the type of HMO. For example, some lenders insist that you can only have up to six occupants all on one tenancy agreement.

(ii) You can get commercial mortgages on an HMO where the value of the property and lending is based on the income the property generates.

33. Question: What type of tenants are the best tenants?

Answer: A difficult one. Very few landlords have had the range of tenants I have had so can rarely compare the differences. If you ask other HMO landlords, they usually say the tenants they are letting to are the best. Each category of tenant – professionals, workers, students and the unemployed – has their advantages and disadvantages. The easiest to deal with in my experience and in this order are professionals, workers and then students. You need to know what you are doing if you house the unemployed: they can be the most difficult to handle, yet some of my very best (and worst) tenants are the unemployed. If you want to know more on letting to the unemployed, see my book 'An Introduction to Letting to The Unemployed for HMO Landlords', available from hmodaddy.com. In practice, HMO landlords let to those they want to deal with.

34. Question: What is the minimum amount of units you would need to make an HMO profitable?

Answer: It depends on what it costs to buy and convert, but for a reasonably priced property, costing around £100k to £150k, I work out that the first four rooms pay bills and the fifth and subsequent rooms provide the profit.

35. Question: How do you advertise for tenants cost effectively?

Answer: Use the web. Most HMO landlords who house professionals, working tenants and students do this. For unemployed tenants, the cheapest way to advertise is to put signs in the windows of your HMO and cards in shop windows, and register with the council, though I am finding a lot of unemployed tenants are now using the web as well.

36. Question: What is the best way to manage HMOs?

Answer: It is best to manage your HMO by yourself. However bad you think you will be you will be far better than an agent as you have the self-interest. You will also make so much more money as you will save on their fees and other costs. For more information on how to run an HMO, get my manual 'HMO Landlords Operating System' available from hmodaddy.com. This explains in detail how to run a HMO.

AUTHORITIES

37. Question: Who, if anyone, do you have to inform if you change your house into a HMO?

Answer: Nobody, if it is not a licensable HMO, as long as you don't exceed six tenants and you are not in an Article 4, selective or additional licensing area (for more on these see Questions 38, 39 &44). Whether you wish to engage with your council is up to you. Most HMO landlords will not have anything to do with their council.

38. Question: Do you need planning permission to convert a house into a HMO?

Answer: You don't need planning permission to convert a

house into an HMO unless there are more than about six tenants or rooms. The exception is in an Article 4 area (see Question 44) where you are required to have planning permission if you house three or more unrelated tenants. For more on this get my book 'Planning and HMOs' available from hmodaddy.com.

39. Question: What is an HMO licence and when does it apply?

Answer: The government has decreed that all three storey or more HMOs must be licensed if there are five or more tenants sharing a kitchen or bathroom. There is little logic to licensing, but you must comply as there is an excessive fine and other penalties apply if you do not. You only need to apply once you let to the fifth tenant, and you do not require a licence before you let. To apply, you have to fill in a lengthy form, provide certificates and floor plans and pay a fee. Many councils see this as an opportunity to raise money.

40. Question: Is an HMO licensable?

Answer: For the majority, no (see answer to Question 39 above). In some areas where the councils have introduced selective or additional licences, you do need a licence. Check with your council to see if additional or selective licensing applies, as in areas of selective or additional licensing all

HMOs, irrespective of size, have to be licenced.

41. Question: How do I work out how many storeys there are? Do you include basements or shops/commercial premises below a flat?

Answer: With a house, all habitable floors count as storeys. This causes a problem for you if you own a house with an accessible cellar and loft, even if not used, as some councils will say they could be habitable, while other councils will ignore them. If I were dealing with an anti-landlord council I would either ask for their opinion in writing or seal off the cellar and loft just to be on the safe side.

There are strange rules concerning flats: all floors of the flat count as storeys, plus you must add to this the commercial or shop floors.

To illustrate the position with flats, I will give you some examples:

a. A one storey flat is not licensable whatever floor it is on, providing there is no commercial element on any floor, if there is see below (d)

b. A two storey flat is not licensable whatever floor it is on; unless there is a commercial premises or a shop on any floor, then it will be licensable.

35

c. A three storey flat is licensable, though I have never come across a three storey flat.

d. A one storey flat is not licensable above a commercial premises or a shop whatever floor it is on unless the commercial premises or shop is more than one storey.

You should also appreciate that an exclusive entrance is treated as a floor, so a flat above a shop where the occupier has their own entrance on the ground floor will be treated as two storeys. If the flat is two storeys it will be caught (i.e. licensable) in two ways: it is a two storey flat and as it is above a shop it will count as a storey and/or it is three storeys as you count the entrance as a floor.
Yes, I agree it makes very little sense and I understand if you now have a headache and need to lie down!

42. Question: When do you need to apply for an HMO licence: before or after tenants move in?

Answer: To be licensable, a property must have three or more storeys, five or more tenants, and any element of a shared kitchen or bathroom. My understanding is that the property is not licensable until you have five tenants, but I don't think any council will care if you license a property before tenants move in if you intend to let it to five tenants in the future. There are draconian penalties if you fail to

36

licence, and if you are in an area that is hot on licensing and prosecuting landlords, it may be sensible to do so beforehand as it could easily be overlooked when the fifth tenant moves in. You do not need to have received the licence to let to five or more tenants, you just need to have applied.

43. Question: How much does an HMO licence cost?

Answer: This varies from a few hundred to over a thousand pounds depending on the council. It usually takes over twelve months to issue a licence and it lasts for five years (six if you count the year it usually takes the council to issue it). Most councils are very slow in issuing licences, but remember you do not need the licence to start to let, you need only to have applied once you have five or more tenants.

44. Question: What rules apply to an HMO in an Article 4 area?

Answer: Article 4 means that a council has withdrawn the general permission to allow up to six people sharing. They must follow a special procedure and give notice before doing this. The result is you are required to apply for planning permission if you wish to let an HMO in an Article 4 area, but oddly there is no penalty if you do not. The most that planners can do is ask you to apply for planning permission, or, if they can show you are causing serious harm, then they can take enforcement action against you that you can appeal. It is only when the enforcement order has expired that it becomes a criminal offence to let your HMO, and you are usually given generous time to evict your tenants. Essentially, if you start an HMO in an Article 4 area and you are not stopped, you are okay. It gets better. Depending on the type of HMO, after four or ten years as you get established use, which means you are immune from enforcement action – see my book 'Planning and HMOs' available from hmodaddy.com.

45. Question: Are there restrictions as to where you can operate an HMO?

Answer: Apart from Article 4 areas (see Question 44 above) and the need to licence if appropriate (see Question 42), there are no restrictions as to where you can operate an HMO. However, if a council was so minded they could, by being very pedantic, make your life so difficult that it wouldn't be worth being an HMO landlord (see Question 48 below).

46. Question: How long do you have to get the property back to its original condition should a planning enforcement order be made?

Answer: Should an enforcement action be taken and you appeal, which you should always do, the Tribunal will usually give a reasonable time to evict the tenants. Unless any other order is given, evicting the tenants is all you need to do. Planning is generally all about how a building is being used and not about the structure or the building. If a building has been built or extended without planning permission, then the Tribunal can order the building or extension is removed.

47. Question: What number of tenants would trigger planning permission?

Answer: Apart from an Article 4 area (see Question 44 above), then it is likely that you would need planning permission with well over six tenants. Like so much to do with HMOs, the answer is not that clear cut. Most planners say you need planning permission if you have more than six tenants, but the law is not that clear. For more see my book 'Planning and HMOs'.

48. Question: Are there different rules and regulations for different parts of the country regarding HMOs?

Answer: Apart from Scotland and Wales which have made their own rules, there shouldn't be different rules and regulations for different areas of the country regarding

HMOs. However, there are about 340 different councils in England and each takes a different approach, ranging from total indifference to support to outright hostility. If you are in an anti HMO area, every rule the council can think of or dream up will be used. I believe an HMO can only exist with the acquiescence of the council. If a council was so minded, they could make operating an HMO unviable or you would have to be very thick skinned and litigious to survive.

49. Question: Why bother putting kitchenettes into rooms if it is going to cause an issue with planning?

Answer: Because tenants want it. You are not housing planners, you are housing tenants, and if you want to attract or keep them, you need to give them what they want.

50. Question: How can a tenant find out if the HMO needs/has a licence?

Answer: Most are put up to it I believe by the Council or a malicious third party. Tenants should be highly motivated to find out whether the HMO has a licence because not having a licence allows the court to make a rent repayment order to the tenant of the rent paid in the last 18 months. In other words, the tenant can get the rent they paid for 18 months refunded. I'm surprised more tenants have not taken more landlords to court over this issue. I like to think it's because most landlords have good relationships with their tenants and people will not usually sue people they like, but the same goes for those they fear. I know plenty of landlords who don't comply with the law and get away with it, and I do wonder how they do.

51. Question: Do I have the right to appeal against licensing decisions that I believe are unreasonable?

Answer: You can generally appeal against any decision imposed by your council. However, you need to know what the law is and what is only wishful thinking by your Council. For example, the law says you must have a bathroom for every five tenants. If you appeal against this, you will lose. However, you may have a good chance winning your appeal if your council insist on a bathroom for every single tenant or every three tenants. Most of what councils usually demand is wishful thinking and is not wanted by either the tenant or the landlord, so it is always worth considering appealing.

52. Question: Can I enter the HMO at any time?

Answer: Yes and no. You have a duty to manage your HMO, so you must check it on regular occasions. How often you should check your HMO has never been defined: I check mine every week, but I am overcautious. Unless it is an emergency, it could be considered unreasonable to enter the property late at night. On the other hand, you do not want to upset your tenants, so if they do not like you turning up unannounced then don't - unless they are up to no good.

53. Question: What do you have to do to a house or a flat to turn it into an HMO?

Answer: There are over 20 things you should do or provide in a property before letting as a HMO. However, what you have to do and to what extent has a lot to do with what your council wants to focus on. To cover the 20 or so things you may be required to do would be a small book in itself. The main items you need to concentrate on are fire detection and safety, gas and electricity safety, certification, and an ownership notice. I have covered all these things and a lot more in my extensive manual 'How to Become a Multimillionaire HMO landlord' available from hmodaddy.com.

54. Question: I understand that one reason for adding a kitchen to each room (making a studio) is the option of converting the original kitchen to another room. Also, I understand from my local authority that council tax is charged per property when the property has a shared kitchen, but on a per room basis when there is no shared kitchen. Do you find the same with your local authority? And is the aggregate cost of Council Tax per room approximately the same as the cost of Council Tax for the whole house if it had a shared kitchen?

Answer: There is no consistency throughout the country as to the charge for Council Tax for HMOs from my experience. Some councils I believe charge Council Tax on a room while others don't charge Council Tax unless asked, even if the room is self-contained i.e. has its own en suite and kitchen, providing the kitchen is in the room and not in a separate room. In other words, some councils let who pays council tax be a voluntary matter.

As I understand it, councils are free to charge Council Tax on a 'dwelling', and the definition of what is considered a dwelling (sometimes also called a 'heridiciment') is very wide, so in effect it is up to a council to decide whether or not they can charge Council Tax on a room. With most HMOs, the property comprises of, or a mixture of:

1) Room with shared kitchen and bathroom

2) Room with own kitchen and shared bathroom

3) Room with shared kitchen and own en suite

4) Room with own kitchen and en suite (self-contained)

The further you move from (1) above, the more likely it is

that the council will band each room separately, but even in (4) above it is not always the case that it will be classified as a dwelling. Some councils will want to see a property with a bathroom and more than one room and a separate kitchen before they will classify it as a dwelling, but again it is all down to the individual council.

With regards to the cost, I do not understand your maths. Unless the Council Tax charge for different bands varies enormously in your area. It will always cost in total far more to have each unit separately banded, even though most tenants will be able to claim the 25% single person discount as they live by themselves. Appreciate that the lowest council charge is band A and this will be charged for a whole house and for a room in an HMO if the room is separately banded.

It can be to the landlord's advantage to have every room separately banded if they house only unemployed tenants as the council pay all or most of the Council Tax for unemployed tenants.

Example: For a property with six rooms in my area, I pay about £1k in Council Tax pa for the whole house. If each room is separately banded for CT, then it will be 6 x £1k x 75% i.e. 4.5 times the cost of the house.

Usually, the only difference is that the landlord pays for the whole HMO or is legally responsible for the Council Tax, but the tenant pays and is usually legally responsible for the Council Tax if the room is separately banded.

In my area, the councils generally charge the landlord Council Tax on HMOs irrespective of whether it is (1) (2) (3) or (4) above, unless the landlord or some idiot tenant requests separate banding.

PROPERTY STANDARDS

55. Question: What are the building regulations for an HMO?

Answer: Unless it is a new build HMO, most councils don't usually require any special building regulations for a house or flat converted into an HMO apart from fire safety i.e. fire alarms and occasionally fire doors. Building control don't normally become involved with a conversion of a house into an HMO. This is because it is mainly only conversions that require structural alterations that need building control approval, and building control usually treats HMOs as a normal houses. However, I have known some over the top building inspectors demand, when asked by a naive landlord, that they apply for Building Control approval, and that each room is soundproofed - so it is best not to involve them. Soundproofing is an expensive and difficult job.

56. Question: Do you need a fire alarm in an HMO?

Answer: Since the October 1st 2015 there is a legal requirement that every storey of a building occupied for residential accommodation under a tenancy or licence is fitted with a smoke detector. Additionally, landlords must prove that the detectors are tested between lets. In any HMO you need adequate fire protection and equipment. What is adequate all depends on your council, i.e. smoke detectors, fire alarm, fire blankets etc. Most councils demand that the detectors are mains operated and interconnected, and others want every room to have a detector (except bathrooms) and so on.

The problem is that the issue only usually comes to light when there is a fire. If someone is injured then the fire service looks to prosecute the landlord, and some landlords have been heavily fined or even sent to prison when it is discovered there is no fire detection equipment.

Strictly speaking, it's up to the landlord both at common law and by the Housing Act to provide adequate fire protection and equipment. Most landlords rely on the council or fire service to make the assessment of how much protection is needed for their HMO, and most councils and fire services are happy to do so for no charge. Understandably, they tend to go over the top, but in such circumstances I always do what they ask even though I don't always think it's completely necessary. Being over the top with fire safety usually keeps the council happy, and it is always best to have a good relationship with your council and be on the safe side should anything go wrong.

57. Question: Do I need to fit fire doors with self-closers and intumescent seals to every door?

Answer: It is down to your council, although strictly speaking the responsibility for deciding whether to or not to fit fire doors is down to the landlord. Most landlords follow the advice of their council. Whenever I fit a door, I fit a fire door, as they are cheap if you shop around. Fire doors are very strong and provide good soundproofing. I would always recommend that you fit fire doors starting with kitchen if refurbishing, but whether you need to is questionable. However, with fire it is always best to err on the side of safety. The exception is bathrooms; they do not need to have a fire door as they are considered a low risk room.

58. Question: Do smoke detectors need to be fitted? Should they be hardwired or can they be battery operated? How many, and where are you supposed to position them?

Answer: I would go beyond the minimum legal requirement introduced by the 'The Smoke and Carbon Monoxide Alarm (England) Regulations 2015' and fit a smoke detector in every room (not just on each floor) and a heat detector in the kitchen. Most councils will want them hardwired and to sound together. I never compromise on fire safety just in case anything goes wrong, and if you know how it is not that expensive to do.

59. Question: Should an HMO be fitted with emergency lighting? How and where should it be located?

Answer: This is down to the council. Because emergency lighting is so cheap, I fit them to all the corridors. I fail to see the point of this lighting in a small HMO, but it keeps the council happy. You could argue against fitting them if there is sufficient light to see in the dark, but I wouldn't skimp.

60. Question: As you are the expert, what fire protection do you insist be in an HMO?

Answer: I am not an expert on fire safety, though I have studied the subject but it is not my opinion that matters. Personally I believe very little fire protection on a risk basis is required other than a few smoke detectors and what my tenants want and will pay for. I find that being over the top on safety tends to negate other failings like a lack of planning, and if you get it wrong and fit too little you leave yourself liable to criminal prosecution and civil liability, so I long ago gave up the argument over fire protection in HMOs.

If you have to fit fire protection (which on a risk basis I do not believe is necessary for an average HMO), I would fit smoke detectors and sprinklers. If some of the standards for fire sprinklers were reduced, the fitting would be easy and cheap. There has never been a death by fire in a fully sprinkled property. Sprinklers also reduce injury from fire and property damage. They are very unlikely to go off by accident causing damage. I find it very strange that the fire service do not insist on sprinklers instead of fire doors and fire resistant escape routes.

LETTING TO THE UNEMPLOYED

61. Question: Does the tenant have to inform you if they are claiming housing benefit?

Answer: No, nor are the council able to tell you unless the tenant consents. A term in your tenancy agreement could require them to inform you, but a tenancy agreement is in practice impossible to enforce against unemployed tenants.

62. Question: How much will housing benefit pay for a tenant, and how do you go about getting extra rent to make it up to what I charge for rent?

Answer: The rent is set by what is known as the Broad Market Rent for an area. You can find this out by going onto the council website. There is nothing to stop a landlord charging whatever rent they want, but with unemployed tenants, just as with other tenants, you need to be sensitive to the market rate. Often you may not be able to get any more than the Broad Market Rate.

We charge all our tenants extra. It is called a 'top up', and for under 25-year-olds we find that whatever you charge you will not get more than £5pw extra. With over 25-year-olds, we can get no more than £15pw extra. Both have to be collected to start with on a fortnightly basis when the tenants receive their giro, otherwise it is spent. Once the tenant has got into the habit of paying, about 40% to 50% will pay automatically. We can rarely get more than 75% of our tenants to pay their 'top up'.

Authors Note: Please do not attempt to let to the unemployed unless you know what you are doing. Though most are genuine, there is a small minority who I have discovered to my cost will destroy your business. The housing benefit system can also be a nightmare. I have written a book 'Introduction to Letting to the Unemployed for HMO Landlords', and I am also in the process of writing a comprehensive manual on the subject. Both are available from hmodaddy.com.

EVICTIONS

63. Question: How do you evict a problem tenant?

Answer: Quickly. If verbal persuasion doesn't work, I try financial incentives, and at the same time I serve a Section 8 notice (usually for rent arrears and a problem tenant almost always has rent arrears). For more on eviction, see my manual DIY Eviction available from hmodaddy.com. Be very careful to not appear to harass the tenant as you could be sued. Harassment seems to be anything that upsets the tenant.

64. Question: How do you evict a non-paying tenant?

Answer: See Question 63 above

65. Question: How much does an eviction cost?

Answer: £250 if you do it yourself. The court costs for

eviction have increased since April 2015 from £100 to £250: a massive increase. It is now well worth giving the tenant a financial incentive to leave the property, and often this is far cheaper in the long run as the tenant is unlikely to be paying the rent during the months it takes to evict them. If you use a solicitor it can cost you well over £2,000 to evict a tenant, and my experience of using solicitors has not been good.

66. Question: How often have you personally had to evict a tenant?

Answer: It used to be about three to five times a week, mostly via persuasion and about once a week through the courts, but this has substantially reduced to less than once a month via the courts. I think this is because we are coming out of the recession and I am letting to fewer problem tenants (i.e. the unemployed), but appreciate that I have over 900 tenants. If I had only 50 tenants (the average number of tenants HMO landlords have), it would equate to a court eviction every other year.

67. Question: How many problem tenants do you have?

Answer: Less than 1% and yes I know it is a very small number, but those tenants take up an enormous amount of time and energy. One bad tenant has on too many occasions cleared a whole house of good tenants and infected other

HMOs I have in the area. The law gives little protection to the landlord in such cases; it is all one way, protecting the tenant. Some of those undesirables know their rights only too well and councils and tenancy support bodies are often very keen to support such people.

68. Question: How often does an eviction go to court?

Answer: Once the process has started, most of my evictions end up in court. If I have paid for a possession hearing, I always go through the process and get a court order. The majority of tenants will leave voluntarily if asked nicely, but I have begun to see an increasing number who go through the whole process.

When I started, most would leave on receipt of a Section 8 Notice. This costs nothing to do: see my manual 'DIY EVICTION' for more information available from hmodaddy.com. Now more and more soon-to-be evicted tenants are waiting for the bailiff's letter. Who can blame them? They're advised by the council and legal advice centres to do this while not paying any rent, and this means that the landlord inevitably incurs the cost of both the eviction and the lost rent. It is thought by many that this is a back door way in which councils can attack and try to destroy the private sector.

69. Question: When evicting, would you recommend settling out of court?

Answer: Yes, I would always rather the tenant leave voluntarily, and I even very reluctantly occasionally give them some financial incentive. It costs £250 to take a tenant to court for eviction, and that doesn't include the solicitor's costs. Because of this, I would consider learning how to evict yourself. I cover all this in my manual 'DIY Eviction' available from hmodaddy.com.

MONEY AND PAYMENTS

70. Question: What is the minimum amount of money you can get per room?

Answer: It all depends on your local area. In my area we get £60 to £80 per week per room (sometimes more) and this is one of the lower cost areas. In the South East you can get well over twice this in rent.

71. Question: What is the minimum amount of money you can get per studio?

Answer: It all depends on your local area. In my area we get £90 to £120 per studio per week and again this is in a lower cost area. In the South East you can get double these rents or even more.

72. Question: How do you get the rent money from unemployed tenants?

Answer: You need to set the method of payment correctly at the start. "A stitch in time saves nine" is very true in this respect. For more, see my manual 'An HMO Landlord's Guide to Letting to Unemployed Tenants'.

73. Question: Are there any extra ways of making money from my HMOs?

Answer: Yes, there are several. You can charge an administration fee, charge for electricity, and charge for use of the washing machine. For more on these and others, please see my fantastic book '35 Money Making Saving Tips for HMO Landlords' available from hmodaddy.com.

INVESTMENT STRATEGIES

Question 74 - 90 talk about my Joint Venture deals.

74. Question: How long will it take to get my money back out of the HMO property I have invested in?

Answer: With a good wind, it will take you one month to purchase, three months to convert, one month to fill with tenants and apply for valuation, and one month to remortgage: six months minimum.

75. Question: Do I need to have a large available sum of money to invest in an HMO?

Answer: In my area I estimate it costs around £100k to

purchase a small HMO, and about £200k to £300k for a large HMO. However, you can now borrow most of this by either getting a development loan or bridging finance.

76. Question: Am I going to make money?

Answer: Nothing is guaranteed, but everyone so far has both made money and managed where they have wanted to recover the money they've invested in buying and renovating the property. Please get my free 'JV Pack' from my website which gives examples of the deals I have done.

77. Question: Will professional people want to stay in an HMO?

Answer: Now we are out of the recession most of my lets are to workers. From four in 10 lets to workers; I now currently let nine in 10 of my HMOs to workers, and this is increasing. I suspect that very soon all of my lets will be to workers, and there will be very few lets to the unemployed.

78. Question: What's it going to cost to provide an HMO and how much am I going to get out of it?

Answer: That all depends on how much you want and have to invest. The bigger the HMO, the more money there is to be made. Please contact rachel@hmodaddy.com and request a free copy of the 'Joint Venture Pack' which will give you a lot more detail.

79. Question: How can you guarantee that I can refinance and get my money back?

Answer: There are no guarantees and there have been a few cases where I have not got all my money back out first time. However, I have when I have later remortgaged. If you JV with me, you will receive 100% of all income until ALL monies have been returned in full: this is my guarantee. "Property for nothing, money for free!"

80. Question: How much of the property does HMO Daddy own?

Answer: We share everything 50/50.

81. Question: What does the 12% management fee cover?

Answer: Please see the management agreement. Essentially, the management fee covers the day-to-day management. As it is deducted as an expense, it is shared 50/50, so in effect it only costs the JV partner 6%.

82. Question: How are bills and insurance sorted/dealt with for the joint venture property?

Answer: The administration of this is covered in the management fee. It makes it a lot easier if we have control: we can set utilities up in the management company name and arrange direct debits so there is no chasing from either side. Bills will be paid using the rental income; the profit left after bills have been paid is split 50/50 between the JV partner and HMO Daddy.

83. Question: I have £250k available and I would want HMO Daddy to source and do everything. What can I get per year as my share of the pre-tax share, allowing for a decent level of upkeep maintenance?

Answer: At a push, with this amount you could carry out two big deals per year (eight to sixteen bed HMOs). After about a year you could be earning about £40k pa, but you would have to be very quick in deciding and responding to your solicitor and lender if you are to do two deals a year. Indecision is the major cause of hold ups. Remember this £40k is on top; you will still have your £250k as it is recovered by remortgaging the property so you could repeat the process and so in two years, if the market holds up, you could be making £80k per annum and so on.

84. Question: Do we share the income 50/50 when HMO Daddy manages the HMO?

Answer: A 12% management fee is charged by me in addition to the 50/50 profit split. This comes out of the gross profits, which means you only pay 6%.

85. Question: If we fail to get all the money I spent back, how does the profit share work and how does the equity that remains get awarded?

Answer: If you fail to get all your money out the deal, my guarantee is that you will receive all profit until all monies are returned without interest. The equity is shared equally.

86. Question: Is it acceptable on any of these deals for the JV partner to finance the purchase via bridging?

Answer: Yes, but the cost of bridging or other finance sources comes out of the JV's share of profit. Be warned: bridging is very expensive and risky.

87. Question: When the property requires repair, are the costs of the repairs split 50/50? If not, who covers these costs?

Answer: When the property requires repair, I would initially pay for the repair work. However, this would be deducted out of the rental income. I make a blanket allowance of £1,000 pa for a small HMO and £2,000 pa for a large HMO to cover incidental repairs as this saves a lot of administration.

88. Question: If I were to invest the full monies for 50% equity, what does HMO Daddy provide to justify the 50% equity share? Also, is the equity share negotiable?

Answer: The equity or profit share is not negotiable. We find the property, assist with purchase, provide builders, supervise building works, advertise, and let the property, as well as manage and maintain the property thereafter.

Once the money is invested and property renovated, my management deal with all the administration such as lettings, tenancy agreements, rent, bills, maintenance etc.

We do all the work, you just sign the cheque with a guarantee that you will get all your investment back out or you keep all the profit until you do.

89. Question: If I'm not eligible for a mortgage/remortgage, should I invest my own funds? Will the deal still go ahead? If I invest my own funds, who will own the equity?

Answer: If this were the case, then I would discuss with you to find out what you want out of the deal. However, I have never come across someone who will JV with me who is isn't eligible for a mortgage.

90. Question: What information do you need to get me a preapproved mortgage before buying?

Answer: Before you invest in a JV, I get you pre vetted by the lender to see if they will lend to you. It doesn't guarantee that you will receive finance, but I have never seen a lender renege once they agreed to lend. The lenders want a lot of information from you including income and expenditure, net worth, employment details, and up to six month's of bank statements.

91. Question: Is it possible to buy a property with a standard buy-to-let mortgage and then remortgage it once the property has been converted and occupied?

Answer: Yes, if the lender allows you to do this.

92. Question: How much can I borrow and what will it cost?

Answer: The sky is the limit with commercial mortgages. Most lenders will lend up to 70% of the investment value.

The cost of borrowing is about 5% to 6% above base giving a pay rate of £5,000 pa to £6,000 pa per £100k borrowed. All lenders are insisting on a repayment mortgage on loans over ten years, giving a pay rate of around £8,000 pa to £10,000 pa per £100k borrowed, because the capital repayment along with interest is included in the payment.

MAINTENANCE

93. Question: Do you use a particular type of complete extraction/air recycling fan system for your HMOs? I believe there are systems that can be installed in the loft that keep the risk of damp and mould to a minimum.

Answer: I generally provide 24/7 background central heating for most of my properties and rarely have condensation issues. I have been warned about the air recycling systems as they have enormous problems in practice. I would love to know how you get on with such system should you try them. My view is that most of the energy conservation measures do not work in practice and the business is a con. It will turn out to be one of the major miss-selling scandals of this century.

94. Question: How often does an HMO require

maintenance? How much does this cost?

Answer: HMOs tend to get a lot of wear and tear. We allow £1,000 a year for a small HMO up to six tenants and an extra £200 pa for every tenant above this number. This does not include large items of expenditure such as re-roofing or major refurbishments. These costs are dealt with as and when. You should appreciate that I do all of my maintenance in house and I employ a fulltime maintenance team. If you were to use outside contractors I suspect it would cost you a lot more. The cheapest way to maintain your HMOs is to do the work yourself; it is also good fun and will save you a lot of money.

95. Question: How often do you visit you HMOs and how do tenants report repairs?

Answer: We have a strict inspection process and the property is checked on a weekly basis. Every room is checked quarterly if the tenant allows us and the property is risk assessed every three months. We provide a phone number that is available 24/7 where tenants can report repairs, and every request is logged and checked to see that it is completed.

96. Question: What is the most common repair reported in HMOs?

Answer: I had my staff do an analysis and surprisingly there is no particular repair that is common. The most troublesome by far, though, are issues with Wi-Fi, central heating not working, and leaks. These issues cause the largest amount of distress to tenants.

97. Question: After seeing your TV programme on the BBC, rooms were trashed and needed a lot of repair work done. Does this occur after each tenant leaves?

Answer: You need to appreciate that what you saw was an edited version of three months filming. The film crew followed me and only picked up on the sensational, although everything apart from the eviction was true. The eviction was staged. All you saw was the exception, which is the very few tenants that trash their rooms. I felt it was all very distorted and I will never believe a documentary again. They bear as much resemblance to the truth as EastEnders does to the life of London Eastender.

98. Question: How often do the HMOs get cleaned, by whom and which areas?

Answer: We have cleaners to clean the communal areas and outside at least once a week, occasionally more often. A room is deep cleaned between lettings. It is the exception that our tenants clean up after themselves.

INSURANCE

99. Question: What levels or types of insurance should someone have on a rent-to-rent business?

Answer: It is up to you. Usually, the owner has the buildings insured. I would always ensure that you have public liability insurance to cover yourself should a tenant try and sue you for injuries received on the property.

100. Question: Do you recommend buildings and contents cover? What do you ensure is covered on insurance?

Answer: I only ever cover buildings, public, and employer liability. I don't feel that house contents are worth insuring.

We tell the tenants to have their own contents insurance. Unfortunately, few do, and they often get very upset when their property is stolen and somehow feel that the landlord is responsible. It is very important to specify who is liable for what on your tenancy agreement.

101. Question: How do you decide what insurer to use?

Answer: I go for the lowest cost insurer, even if it means having a high excess (the amount the insured has to pay should they make a claim).

BONUS QUESTIONS

I like to give exceptional value so here are some bonus questions and answers

Bonus Question 1: I have put kitchenettes into a few of my rooms that also have en suites, thereby achieving the one bedroom housing benefit rate for my unemployed tenants. I have just received a letter from the Local Authority Planning department saying due to sub-division of a dwelling I now need to apply for planning for these self-contained rooms. Do you have to apply for planning for your rooms that have kitchenettes and en suites?

Answer: We claim one bedroom rate for unemployed tenants, but we are clear to point out to the planners, should they get involved, that there are shared facilities, usually a kitchen. If they ask about the kitchenettes in the rooms, we call them 'tea making facilities'. I would suggest that any cookers are moveable i.e. not fitted cookers, oven or hot plates but plug in mini cookers. We have not had any problems so far by doing this. I have, however, on a very few occasions had to explain to the Housing Benefit department the housing benefit rules. Some in the Housing Benefit department try to say that the one bedroom rate only applies to flats or if the tenant is paying their own council tax. I write back and tell them that the regulations state that if the tenant has exclusive use of a kitchen and bathroom they are entitled to the one bed rate. I once had to get the tenant to appeal to the Appeal Tribunal to get the one bedroom and lost over six months' rent as a result.

Bonus Question 2: Why the need for an HMO licence?

Answer: The government line is that bedsits and shared houses (i.e. HMOs) often have poorer physical and management standards than other privately rented properties. The people who live in HMOs are amongst the most vulnerable and disadvantaged members of society. As HMOs are the only housing option for many people, the government recognises that it is vital that they are properly regulated.

Licensing is intended to ensure that:

- Landlords of HMOs are "fit and proper people", or they employ managers who are

- Each HMO is suitable for occupation by the number of people allowed under the licence

- The standard of management of the HMO is adequate

- High risk HMOs can be identified and targeted for improvement.

Where landlords refuse to meet these criteria, the council can intervene and manage the property so that:

- Vulnerable tenants can be protected

- HMOs are not overcrowded.

As you can appreciate, I have different views on the above and there is little evidence to support it or show it makes much difference. I believe it is the landlords who need protection and not the tenants.

Bonus Question 3: Why do HMOs need to be licensed?

Answer: It is compulsory (required by law) to licence a HMO if it is:

1. Three or more storeys high, and

2. Has five or more people in more than one household, and

3. Amenities such as bathrooms, toilets and cooking facilities are shared.

The above sounds very admirable but does not make any sense and there is no evidence to support the argument that three storey buildings are a greater risk. The councils have powers to deal with all HMOs. Just because an HMO is three storeys and licensable does not automatically make it a risk, though it is argued that these types of properties represent a greater fire risk. However, I have not seen and I do not believe there is any current evidence to support this. Licensing is just something to make it appear that the government is doing something to regulate the private sector without any evidence that regulation is needed or provides any benefit. It also creates employment for Housing Standards Officers and revenue via the licence fee for the Councils.

It is not generally appreciated that the same rules apply to a non-licensed HMO as to a licensed HMO: the justifications given by the government also apply to non-licensed HMOs. The only possible advantage to licensing an HMO is that the owner must notify the council i.e. apply for a licence and in all likelihood this is going to be the conscientious landlord. Many landlords sell their three storey buildings, close off the second floor, or limit occupation to below five to avoid licensing.

Be very careful when going down the road of asking 'why' especially if you think about the answers as they rarely stand very much analysis, so much in this business does not make any sense and is a waste of time, money and resources. Worse, most of what is done is grossly one sided against the landlord and pro tenant.

Bonus Question 4: What are permitted development rights?

Answer: Under planning law there are a lot of things that can be done without planning permission. For example, a residential house can be extended within strict limits and buildings erected in the garden without planning permission. The most useful development right from an HMO landlord's point of view is the ability to let to up to six tenants without planning permission. Permitted development rights can be withdrawn by the council e.g. Article 4 Direction (see Question 44), and do not apply in certain circumstances, for example to a Grade I or II building or conservation areas.

PRODUCTS AND SERVICES

Hopefully I have managed to answer your questions. As I have mentioned in the introduction, if there is anything you require answering in more depth or you want to ask a question that is not answered in the book, please do not hesitate to email info@hmodaddy.com where a member of staff will be more than happy to help.

If you are just starting out and would like to learn more, please visit hmodaddy.com and look at the training courses and materials I have available that are guaranteed to help you along your journey as an HMO Landlord.

The End!

Useful contacts at HMO Daddy:

Wayne Morris – wayne@hmodaddy.com
(Marketing manager)

Rachel Tonks – rachel@hmodaddy.com
(Joint venture liaison manager)